T0378935

SCIENTIFIC AMERICAN | EDUCATIONAL PUBLISHING

SCIENTIFIC AMERICAN INVESTIGATES CAREERS IN SCIENCE

AEROSPACE ENGINEER

BY MEGAN QUICK

Published in 2026 by The Rosen Publishing Group
in association with Scientific American Educational Publishing
2544 Clinton Street, Buffalo NY 14224

Cataloging-in-Publication Data
Names: Quick, Megan.
Title: Aerospace engineer / Megan Quick.
Description: Buffalo, New York : Scientific American Educational Publishing, an imprint of Rosen Publishing, 2026. | Series: Scientific American investigates careers in science | Includes glossary and index.
Identifiers: ISBN 9781725352469 (pbk.) | ISBN 9781725352476 (library bound) | ISBN 9781725352483 (ebook)
Subjects: LCSH: Aerospace engineering–Juvenile literature. | Aerospace engineers–Juvenile literature.
Classification: LCC TL793.Q53 2026 | DDC 629.1023–dc23

Designer: Leslie Taylor
Editor: Megan Quick

Portions of this work were originally authored by Zelda Salt and published as *Be an Aerospace Engineer*. All new material in this edition is authored by Megan Quick.

Photo credits: Cover (main) Gorodenkoff/Shutterstock.com; series art (background) jijomathaidesigners/Shutterstock.com; p. 5 Gorodenkoff/Shutterstock.com; p. 7 Summit Art Creations/Shutterstock.com, (inset) Tholly/File:Chinese Kite.jpg_commons.wikimedia.org; p. 8 NASA/Photo/nasa.gov; p. 9 Mechanical Subsystems from Space Shuttle News Reference (NASA)/nasa.gov; p. 10 Digital Images Studio/Shutterstock.com; p. 11 Sipa USA via AP/apnews.com; p. 13 Frame Stock Footage/Shutterstock.com; p. 14 AlexandrBognat/Shutterstock.com; p. 15 Robert Way/Shutterstock.com; p. 16 Photo Veterok/Shutterstock.com; p. 17 Vegorus/Shutterstock.com, (inset) zombiu26/Shutterstock.com; p. 19 Gorodenkoff/Shutterstock.com; p. 21 Gorodenkoff/Shutterstock.com; p. 23 Gorodenkoff/Shutterstock.com; p. 24 Valkantina/Shutterstock.com; p. 25 gorodenkoff/iStockphoto.com; p. 27 Andrei Armiagov/Shutterstock.com, (inset) simon2579/iStockphoto.com; p. 29 NASA Photo/Alamy.com.

Some of the images in this book illustrate individuals who are models. The depictions do not imply actual situations or events.

Printed in the United States of America

CPSIA compliance information: Batch #CSSA26. For Further Information contact Rosen Publishing at 1-800-237-9932.

Find us on

CONTENTS

Words in the glossary appear in **bold** type the first time they are used in the text.

IDEAS TAKING FLIGHT

Have you ever looked up in the sky and wondered how birds and planes fly? Do you like figuring out how things work? Do you enjoy creating and building? A career as an aerospace engineer might be for you.

Engineers take a problem, or a challenge, and figure out how to solve it. They **design** and build new machines or methods for doing things. Aerospace engineers work with airplanes, spacecraft, and **satellites**. They use computers, math, and science to find ways to make flight smoother and safer. Aerospace engineers allow us to travel through the sky and explore what is beyond it.

FUN FACT

NEIL ARMSTRONG IS MOST FAMOUS FOR THE BEING THE FIRST MAN TO STEP FOOT ON THE MOON. BUT YOU MAY NOT KNOW THAT BEFORE HE BECAME AN ASTRONAUT, ARMSTRONG WAS AN AEROSPACE ENGINEER.

A career as an aerospace engineer begins with being curious about space and how things work.

5

MANY JOBS

Aerospace engineering is a broad field. It includes designing, developing, and testing machines for flight. Aerospace engineers work with aircraft, helicopters, spacecraft, rockets, and **drones**. They create new **technologies** for parts and **materials** that will be used in flight, and then they test them over and over again.

Aerospace engineers have a specialty, or an area they spent a lot of time studying. They might focus on **research** and development of systems or materials. They may work on avionics, or the computer systems aircraft use. They might work in testing and maintenance, making repairs and changes. All of these specialty areas are important parts of both astronautical and aeronautical engineering.

Dreams of Flight

People have long been curious about flight. Kites were probably invented in China more than 2,000 years ago. Much later, kites were used as models for early airplanes. Hot air balloons were one of the first ways people experienced flying. The first balloon trip with a person on board took place in 1783.

7

SPACESHIPS AND SATELLITES

Astronautical engineers build spacecraft or other technology that will be used in space. They design, test, and maintain spacecraft and technology that will leave Earth's atmosphere, or the mixture of gases that surround our planet. They also study the **environment** that space-bound technology will have to survive in. For example, astronautical engineers may track space weather patterns.

A strong background in math is necessary for aerospace engineering. Astronautical engineers use math to figure out how a spacecraft will leave Earth's atmosphere, for example. They do this by answering questions about distance, speed, and flight paths—all of which require high-level math skill and knowledge.

Space Shuttle _Endeavour_

Space Shuttle

This drawing shows the many parts of a space shuttle that took astronauts into space. It's an aerospace engineer's job to know all of the names and uses for these parts.

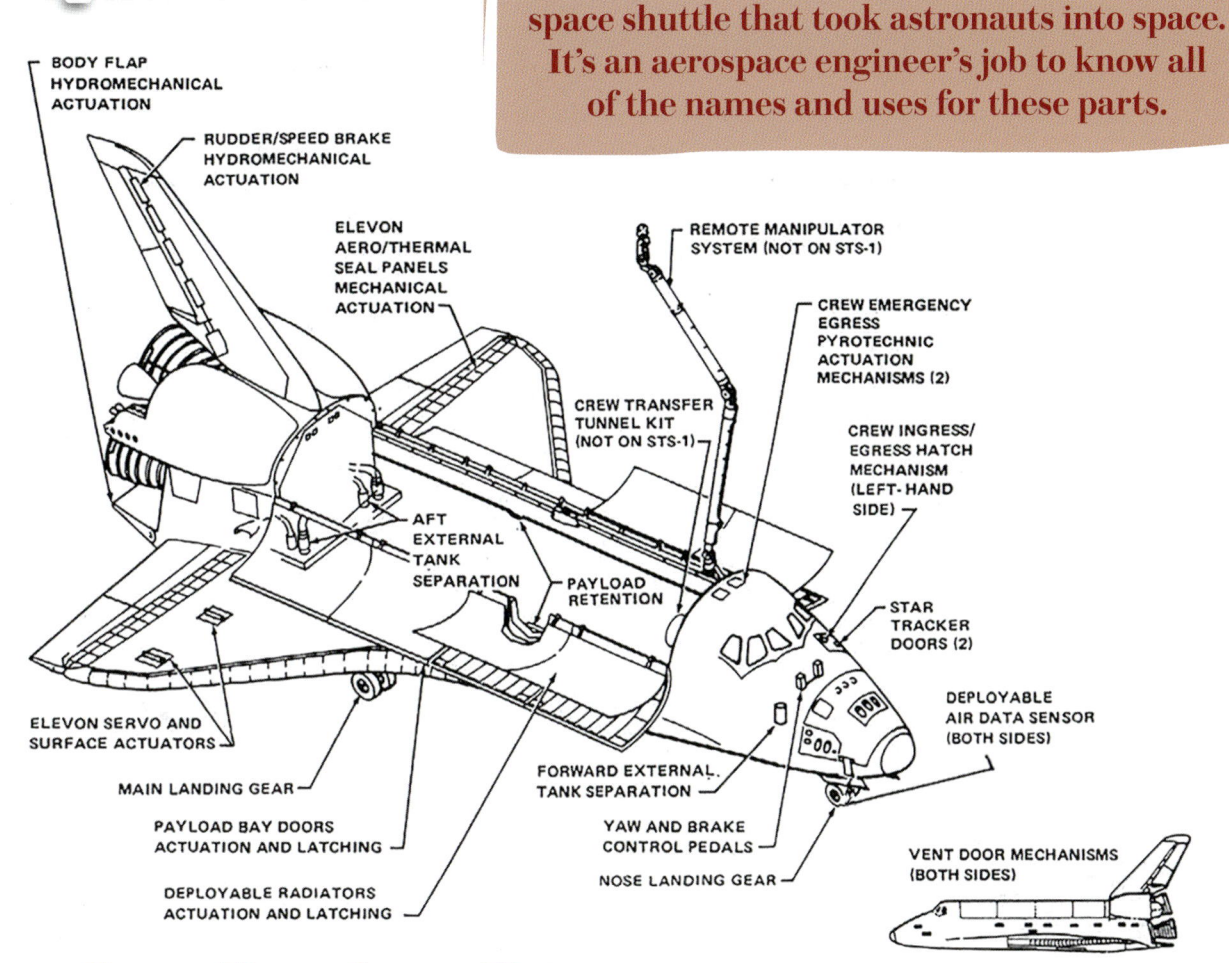

BODY FLAP HYDROMECHANICAL ACTUATION

RUDDER/SPEED BRAKE HYDROMECHANICAL ACTUATION

ELEVON AERO/THERMAL SEAL PANELS MECHANICAL ACTUATION

REMOTE MANIPULATOR SYSTEM (NOT ON STS-1)

CREW EMERGENCY EGRESS PYROTECHNIC ACTUATION MECHANISMS (2)

CREW TRANSFER TUNNEL KIT (NOT ON STS-1)

CREW INGRESS/ EGRESS HATCH MECHANISM (LEFT-HAND SIDE)

AFT EXTERNAL TANK SEPARATION

PAYLOAD RETENTION

STAR TRACKER DOORS (2)

DEPLOYABLE AIR DATA SENSOR (BOTH SIDES)

ELEVON SERVO AND SURFACE ACTUATORS

MAIN LANDING GEAR

PAYLOAD BAY DOORS ACTUATION AND LATCHING

FORWARD EXTERNAL TANK SEPARATION

YAW AND BRAKE CONTROL PEDALS

NOSE LANDING GEAR

VENT DOOR MECHANISMS (BOTH SIDES)

DEPLOYABLE RADIATORS ACTUATION AND LATCHING

Goundbreaking Engineer

In 1958, Mary Jackson became the first Black, female aerospace engineer at NASA (National Aeronautics and Space Administration). It took a lot of hard work for Jackson to get the job. She had to get special permission to attend night classes in engineering. During her time at NASA, Jackson studied how air affects spacecraft.

Astronautical engineers don't just build spacecraft that carry astronauts to space. They also design satellites and build **unmanned** spacecraft. These travel and explore farther than spacecraft with humans aboard. Their work plays an important role in helping scientists make new advances and discoveries in space.

In 2023, a spacecraft delivered samples from a 4.5-billion-year-old **asteroid** to Earth. Astronautical engineers designed the spacecraft so it could reach an asteroid millions of miles away, take samples of rock, and carry those samples back to Earth. The samples will allow scientists to learn more about how life began on Earth and the matter that exists in our solar system.

FUN FACT

APOLLO 11 FIRST LANDED ON THE MOON IN 1969. THERE WERE SIX TOTAL MOON LANDINGS WITH A CREW BETWEEN 1969 AND 1972. THE NEXT LANDING IS SET TO HAPPEN IN 2026.

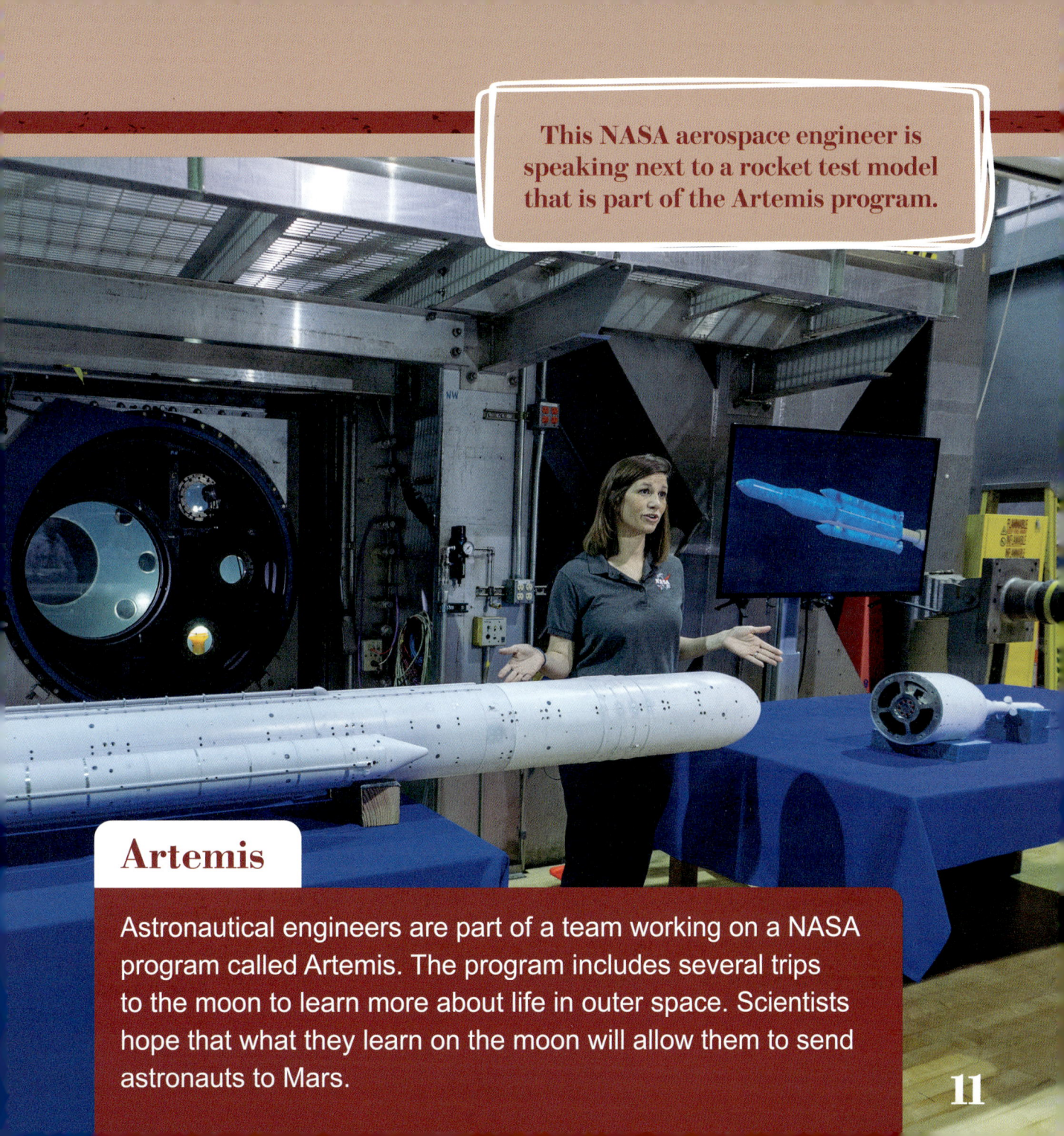

This NASA aerospace engineer is speaking next to a rocket test model that is part of the Artemis program.

Artemis

Astronautical engineers are part of a team working on a NASA program called Artemis. The program includes several trips to the moon to learn more about life in outer space. Scientists hope that what they learn on the moon will allow them to send astronauts to Mars.

DESIGNING AIRCRAFT

The work of aeronautical engineers focuses on aircraft, such as planes, that stay inside Earth's atmosphere. Besides airplanes, aeronautical engineers work with helicopters, drones, and even hot air balloons.

The duties of both aeronautical and astronautical engineers include designing parts, developing technology, and testing aircraft for safety. But there are differences between the two jobs. Perhaps the biggest difference is that there's no air in space. Spacecraft cannot fly the same way that aircraft do. An aeronautical engineer figures out how to use wind to lift an aircraft off the ground. An astronautical engineer must find a way for spacecraft to create their own lift, using engines.

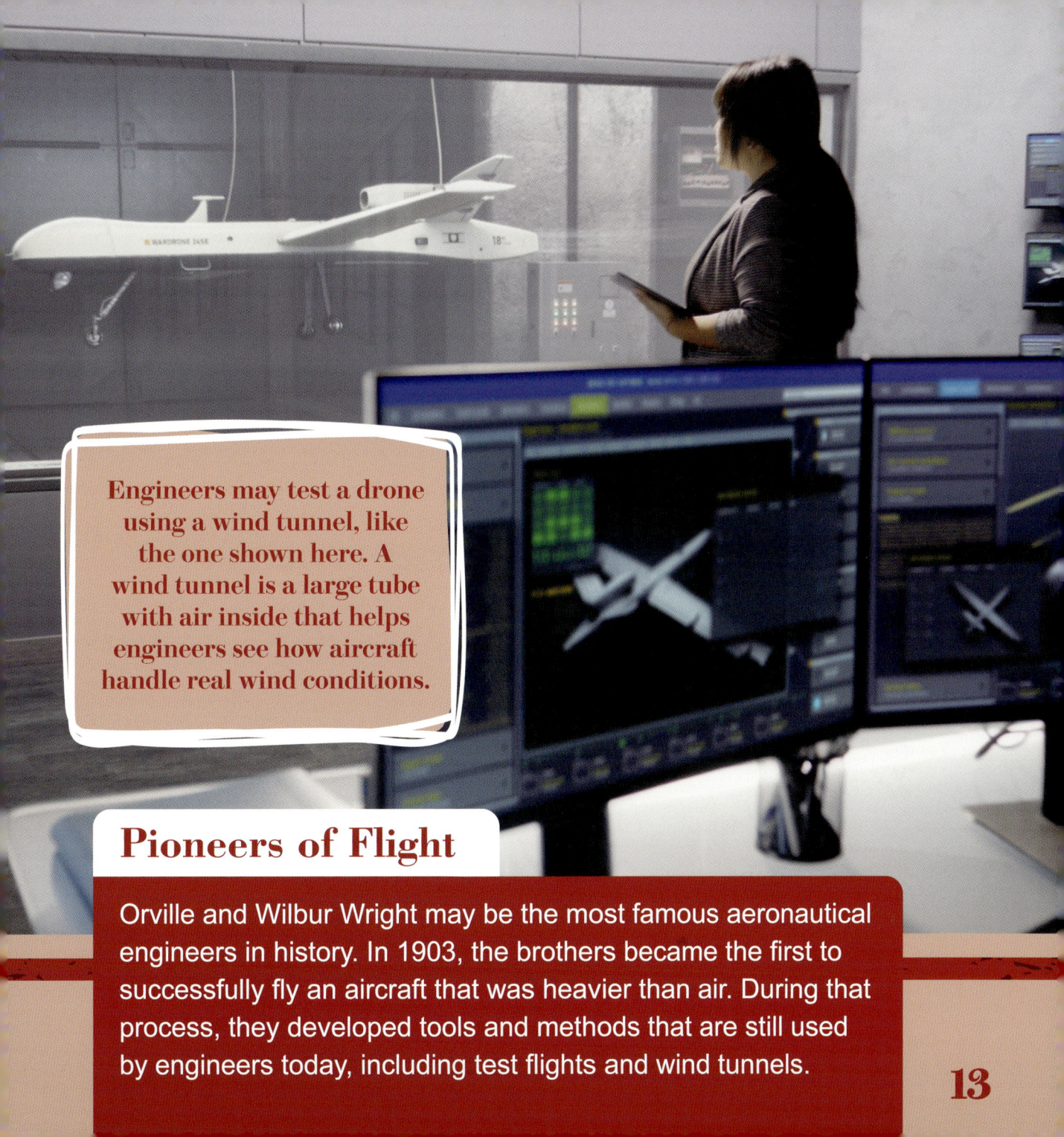

Engineers may test a drone using a wind tunnel, like the one shown here. A wind tunnel is a large tube with air inside that helps engineers see how aircraft handle real wind conditions.

Pioneers of Flight

Orville and Wilbur Wright may be the most famous aeronautical engineers in history. In 1903, the brothers became the first to successfully fly an aircraft that was heavier than air. During that process, they developed tools and methods that are still used by engineers today, including test flights and wind tunnels.

Aeronautical engineers are always looking for ways to improve the performance and safety of different types of aircraft. One major challenge facing aircraft makers is protecting the environment. Airplanes today give off gases that are harmful to life on Earth. Engineers are working to change that.

As of 2024, engineers and scientists at NASA, along with the aircraft company Boeing, were developing a new type of **sustainable** aircraft. This new plane would use less fuel and give off fewer gases into the atmosphere. Engineers plan to accomplish this by using new materials and changing the fuel system as well as the shape of the plane.

FUN FACT

IN THE 1950s, AN AERONAUTICAL ENGINEER NAMED CHARLES ZIMMERMAN CAME UP WITH THE IDEA FOR A HOVERBOARD—A FLYING PLATFORM. HIS IDEA DIDN'T TAKE OFF, BUT ENGINEERS HAVE CONTINUED HIS WORK, AND TODAY HOVERBOARDS DO EXIST.

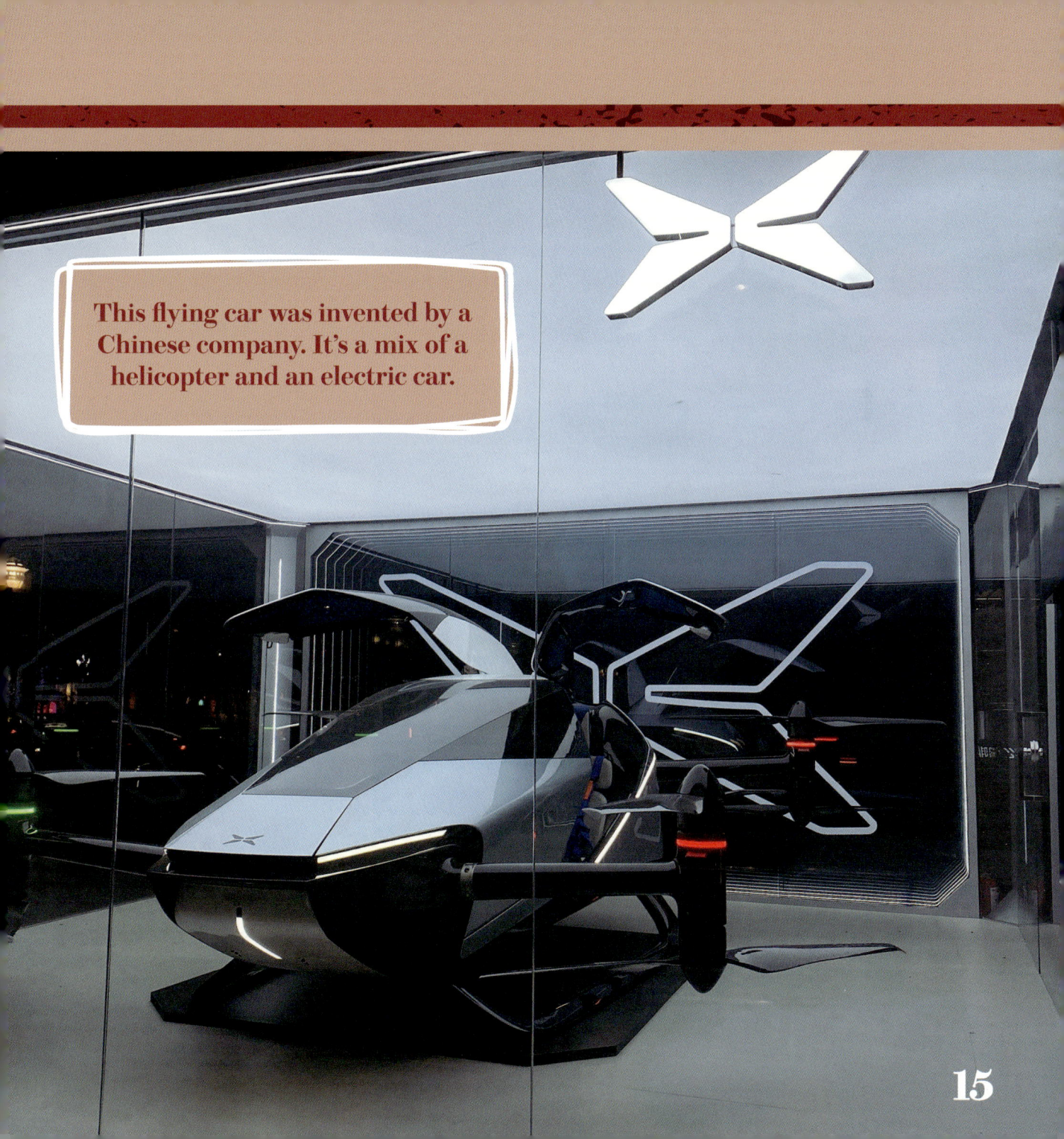

This flying car was invented by a Chinese company. It's a mix of a helicopter and an electric car.

HIT THE BOOKS

If a career in aerospace engineering sounds right for you, you'll need to work hard! You'll want to focus on STEM: Science, Technology, Engineering, and Math. This will mean taking classes in chemistry, physics, and advanced math in high school. When you get to college, you can major in engineering. At some colleges, you can even major in aerospace engineering.

Aerospace engineering classes will cover many details about flight. You'll learn how to plan a path to travel in space and how to make a spacecraft move. You will also have classes on aerodynamics, or how an aircraft or spacecraft interacts with the atmosphere when it flies.

Air Pressure and Flight

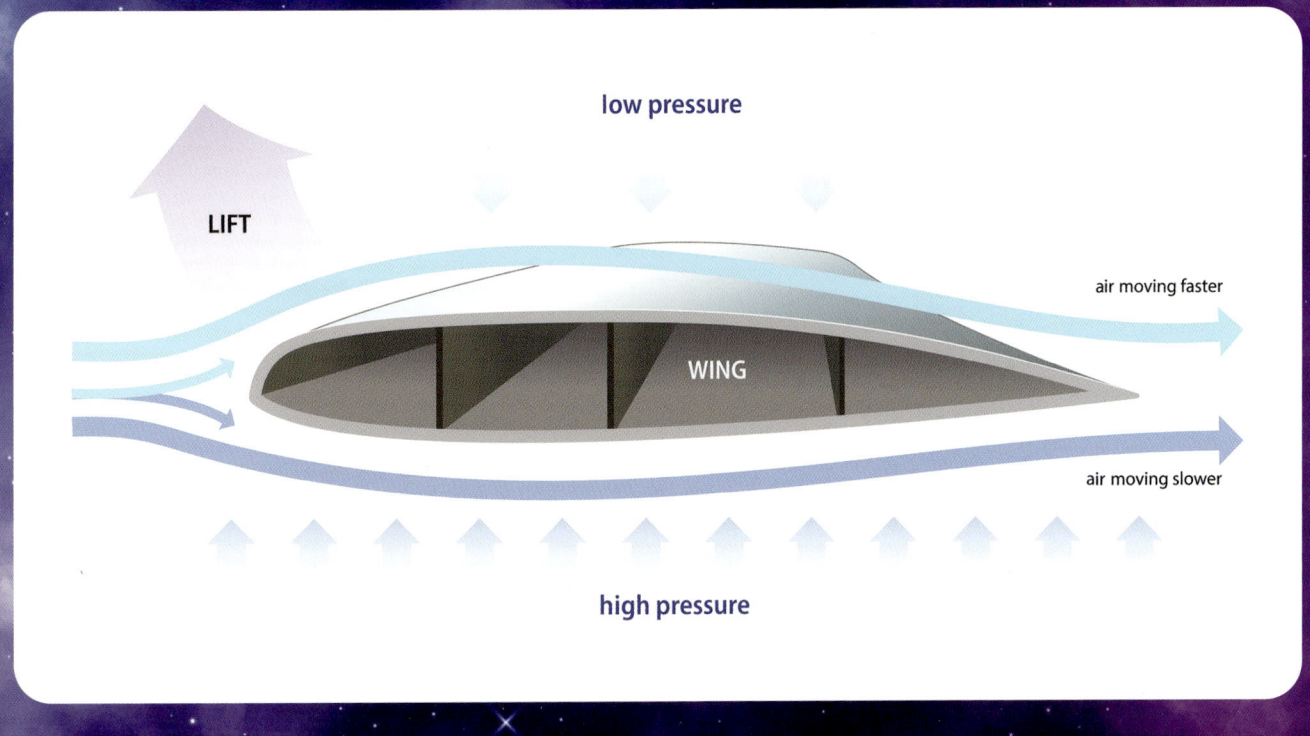

low pressure

LIFT

air moving faster

WING

air moving slower

high pressure

Studying physics is an important step in understanding flight. This diagram shows how the force of air pressure on a plane's wings lifts them up.

NEW LANGUAGES

Have you ever wanted to learn another language? It might help you in your career as an aerospace engineer. Learning a language other than English allows engineers to work for companies in other countries. Some of the biggest aerospace manufacturers are in Russia, France, Italy, China, and the United States. Aerospace engineering students may want to focus on the languages spoken in those areas.

There's also another type of language future engineers may want to learn—programming! Students interested in the technology and computer engineering side of aerospace should take programming classes to learn different ways to code, or write computer programs.

This aerospace engineer is using a computer to track a satellite.

HELP WANTED

Once you have finished school, you'll need to find a job. Who hires aerospace engineers? You might think of NASA first. It's part of the U.S. government and deals with American space organizations, and also works with space groups from other countries.

But the aerospace field is growing quickly. Job opportunities outside of NASA are becoming more widely available. Airlines looking to improve or update their aircraft hire aerospace engineers. Private companies are thinking of how to help more people travel to space. And the military hires a range of aerospace engineers to assist in building and maintaining their aircraft as well as spacecraft.

FUN FACT

DO YOU WONDER HOW MUCH YOU WOULD BE PAID AS AN AEROSPACE ENGINEER? IN 2023, THE AVERAGE PAY WAS JUST OVER $130,000 PER YEAR. THAT'S ALMOST $63 AN HOUR!

Army engineers study a drone that is used to gather information. The military hires aerospace engineers to work on many of its aircraft.

ENGINEERS AT WORK

Once you've gotten a job as an aerospace engineer, what will your days be like? It depends on your specialty, but you'll probably spend a lot of time in an office. You may also work at laboratories, testing sites, airfields, or spaceports. These are sites where spacecraft are launched or land.

As an aerospace engineer, teamwork will be an important part of your job. You might start each day meeting with the other people who are working on the same project. You'll review your goals and give each other updates. You'll trade ideas and come up with plans to meet your goals. Then it's time to get down to work.

A team of aerospace engineers work together to design a jet engine.

Much of an aerospace engineer's work happens at a desk. You may use computer programs to develop blueprints, or plans, for an aircraft or spacecraft. You may also spend time studying **data**, solving **equations**, or writing papers explaining what you've learned. But there's also hands-on work. You might spend time in a workshop or lab, testing and building **prototypes**.

Wherever they work, engineers spend lots of time problem solving. You'll study test results and see where something has gone wrong. On your own or with a team, you'll brainstorm ideas about how to fix problems. If you like solving puzzles, you might enjoy being an engineer!

This engineer is fixing a drone in a laboratory.

SPACE INVENTIONS ON EARTH

Sometimes the inventions dreamed up by aerospace engineers find new uses in our daily lives on Earth. The memory foam that is used in mattresses is one example. NASA engineers first made memory foam when they were trying to find a way to keep pilots safely seated during flight.

You might be surprised to learn that the baby food in your supermarket was created by aerospace engineers. Most of today's baby food contains special nutrients, or ingredients that are important for growth. This soft food was first made for astronauts who were in space for long periods of time.

Satellites in space, like the one shown here, help people on Earth get to where they're going.

FUN FACT

DOES YOUR FAMILY USE A GPS (GLOBAL POSITIONING SYSTEM) APP IN THE CAR? GPS HELPS PEOPLE NAVIGATE, OR FIND THEIR WAY. SPACE SATELLITES, BUILT BY AEROSPACE ENGINEERS, POWER GPS APPS ON CELL PHONES AND IN CARS.

AIM FOR THE STARS

People have been flying planes for just over 100 years. The first person flew into space about 60 years ago. Humans have learned a lot in that time, but there are still many more questions to answer and discoveries to make.

Aerospace engineers think about how we can make these discoveries. They come up with new ideas. They plan, test, and build. It may take a long time, but they turn their ideas into something real. With plenty of hard work, you could become an aerospace engineer and help answer important questions about what lies beyond our planet.

The SLS rocket, carrying the *Orion* spacecraft, lifted off in November 2022 on its way to the moon.

Launching Into the Future

In 2022, NASA launched the world's most powerful rocket. The SLS (Space Launch System) rocket is designed to carry humans past the moon to planets such as Mars, or even deep space. NASA's aerospace engineers designed the rocket to achieve a very strong thrust, or force that pushes a rocket forward.

29

GLOSSARY

asteroid: Any of the small rocky bodies in space found especially between the orbits of Mars and Jupiter.

data: Facts and figures. Also, information created and stored by a computer.

design: To create the pattern or shape of something.

drone: An unmanned aircraft or ship guided by remote control or by computers carried onboard.

environment: The conditions that surround a living thing and affect the way it lives.

equation: A statement of the equality of two mathematical expressions.

material: Matter from which something is made.

prototype: The first model on which later models are based.

research: Careful study and investigation for the purpose of discovering and explaining new knowledge.

satellite: An object that circles Earth in order to collect and send information or aid in communication.

sustainable: Related to using a resource so that the resource is not used up or damaged.

technology: Using science, engineering, and other industries to invent useful tools or to solve problems. Also a machine, piece of equipment, or method created by technology.

unmanned: Having no crew aboard.

FOR MORE INFORMATION

Books

Borgert-Spaniol, Megan. *STEM in the Skies*. Minneapolis, MN: Abdo Publishing, 2024.

Owings, Lisa. *Aerospace Engineer*. Minneapolis, MN: Bellwether Media, 2024.

Reynolds, Donna. *Humans in Space*. Buffalo, NY: Cavendish Square Publishing, 2024.

Websites

Engineer Kids!: Aerospace Engineering
www.engineerkids.org/aerospace-engineering
Get to know real-life aerospace engineers and try out some engineering activities.

NASA: Dynamics of Flight
www.grc.nasa.gov/www/k-12/UEET/StudentSite/dynamicsofflight.html
Learn about the science behind how airplanes and spacecraft fly.

NASA Kids' Club
www.nasa.gov/learning-resources/nasa-kids-club/
Have fun, play interactive games, and learn all about space!

INDEX